167

*A Druid.*

# A COMPLETE HISTORY

of the

# DRUIDS;

THEIR ORIGIN,

Manners, Customs, Powers, Temples, Rites,
and Superstition;

WITH

## *An Inquiry into their Religion,*

And its Coincidence with the

# PATRIARCHAL.

WITH TWO ENGRAVINGS.

LICHFIELD:
PRINTED BY AND FOR T. G. LOMAX;

AND SOLD BY

*Longman, Hurst, Rees, & Orme, London.*

1810.

9407. e 2.

# ADDRESS.

AS it is impossible for Man, even arrived to an age of perfect reason, to recollect what has passed in his infancy, so it is impossible for any nation, though in the highest degree of civilization, to know any thing certain of their origin.

However, the knowledge which is necessary for man to possess, and which, undoubtedly, deserves his most particular care and attention, is that of himself: yet, mankind, in the eyes of the wise, seem divided into two parts; one of unbelievers, endeavouring to darken the light of truth; the other, equally weak in mind, searching for and delighting in idle fables. Such is our natural frailty, that we make probability uncertain, and would have uncertainty probable.

We must not bound our capacity in a less compass than was intended, by the Almighty, whose view in granting it, and placing us amidst the awful wonders of this world, was, no doubt, that we should daily contemplate and reflect on them, to encrease our understanding, improve our heart, make wisdom the sacred rule of our mind, that we may arrive at our short jour-ney's end, worthy the glorious and delightful rest, reserved at his side for the virtuous.

In all ages men have proceeded differently in search of truth, and the knowledge of them-selves; their ideas were so very extravagant, and the various opinions they have had, are altogether so strange to our more enlightened minds, that we cannot view them without the strongest emotions, and the most indignant surprize, at their uniting such savage errors and gross absurdities, with the superiority of the learning they possessed.

A person, who can recal the scenes of ancient days, will not traverse the island of Great Britain, which craft and superstition so long made the theatre of a cruel religion, without feeling eager curiosity, succeeded by a kind of awful horror, in viewing those places, where, in the gloom of the thickest woods, the Druids performed their tremendous rites, where they erected their sanguinary temples, and bathed their altars with the blood of human victims.

The friend of mankind, having viewed with grief these barbarous customs, will rejoice at finding that human fancies and irregular passions are no longer the rule of the new Order of the Druids, now flourishing, in the same parts, under more sound and wise laws.

The object of the following Work, is not to add new matter to the British History, but an impartial relation of transactions curious and entertaining, and to record to posterity this part of our History, of late years so much neglected; it is therefore presumed to be worthy the attention of every Briton.

# INTRODUCTION.

As it will be necessary to give an explanation of the *Pillars*, the *Circle*, and the *Serpent;* we chuse rather to give it by way of Introduction, than to break into the main design, by inserting it in the body of the work.

I. That the *Setting up of Pillars*, was, in the original use and intention, innocent and pious, will appear in the course of this History, from unquestionable authority. This will justify the regard for these pieces of antiquity; for such, particularly as remain in this kingdom; and which were, without doubt, raised by Believers, and never desecrated by idolatrous purposes. For when the Romans introduced their vanities, they brought with them the use of covered temples; and on the perversion of the inhabitants, these open places, in all probability, were entirely neglected, if not partly demolished. They were to be destroyed in the Land of Canaan, because they had been abused there; but how far the Israelites were forbidden to set up any more will best appear from the precept itself: Levit. xxvi. 1. "Ye shall make " you no idols nor graven images, neither shall " you put up any image of stone in your land, " to bow down unto it, for I am the Lord your " God." We need but read the words to be

convinced that idolatry alone was here prohibited. And indeed but a little before, in
Exod. xxiv. 4. we find Moses himself " building
an altar and twelve pillars" unto the true God.
So likewise, long after this prohibition, we are
told, 1st Sam. vii. 12. " Samuel took a stone
" and set it up, and called the name of it Ebe-
" nezer, saying, hitherto hath the Lord helped
" us;" and verse 12, " there built he an altar
unto the Lord;" and chap. x. 3. " Thou shalt
" come to the Plain of Tabor, and shall meet
" thee three men going up to God to Bethel."
Here we find the very same open temple, which
the Patriarch Jacob had raised and consecrated,
resorted to, even in the time of Samuel, for
religious purposes; though it is difficult to con-
ceive how it should have escaped the abuses of
the degenerate Canaanites during the sojourning
in Egypt.

II. The *Circle*, will be allowed an apposite
emblem of that infinity which is applicable
only to the Supreme Being. But the Shemim,
the body of the sun, the light thence issuing,
and the spirit or air in perpetual motion to and
from it, were, from the beginning, the great
natural emblems of the Divine Person: that
the solar body, before writing, could not be
more properly represented than by the figure
of a Circle; by which means it became the ar-
tificial or secondary emblem of the First Person,
and one so plain and inoffensive, that it was
scarcely possible to pervert it to the uses of
idolatry. A still further purpose in the sacred
use of this figure will be found in the Work
itself. It was the only means which they could
devise of expressing that irradiation of glory,

By which the first place of public worship, after the expulsion from Paradise, had been set apart and consecrated to the solemn service of the Divinity. What concerns the Seraph, may require a fuller discussion; as one species of the serpentine kind was instrumental in the fall of man, and a curse was then denounced against it. For, upon this consideration, all imaginable objection to be formed against it must be chiefly founded.

III. This *Serpent* was the symbol of light and wisdom, of life and health, amongst the eastern nations, the Indians, Persians, Babylonians, Phœnicians, Egyptians, Grecians, and if we may believe Joseph Acosta, even amongst the Peruvians; and was thence in religious matters applied to Him, whom they distinguished as the Divine Light; the Wisdom of God; the Giver of Life; and the Saviour of Mankind: To this, several causes might concur; as, the annual renovation of its youth and beauty; its sinuosity, which enabled it to put on various forms; the acuteness of vision, and the extraordinary sagacity ascribed to it; its color, which is that of vivid flame or burnished brass: and the names which it bore.

Its name of Seraph, particularly, is so expressive of that blaze of brightness which it seemed to furnish when reflecting the splendor of the sun-beams; that it has been transferred to a superior order of angels, and is once made use of to denote even the glorious appearance of the Cherubim.

Another name of it, Chevia or Chuia, (though not found in the Bible, yet preserved in the Syriac and Chaldee) has a near affinity

with that which Adam gave to the mother of
mankind, calling her name Cheva, because
she was the mother of all living.

A fragment, written in the Phœnician
tongue, has the word (Chuia) for this serpent,
with an eye to both these meanings, and ex-
plains the entire figure of Abiry. " Jupiter,
" (says the fragment) is a feigned sphere; from
" it is produced a serpent: the sphere shews
" the Divine Nature to be without beginning or
" end; the serpent his word, which animates the
" world and makes it prolific; his wings, the
" Spirit of God, that by its motion gives life to
" the whole mundane system."

But the great reason, (for this includes the
reason of the name also) why they considered it
as an emblem of the solar light, and so as a
substituted one of the second person, was, its
extreme brightness and radiancy, and the very
glorious appearance which it made; for it was
the serpent of the fiery-flying species; the same
sort that we read of in Isaiah, xxx. 6, and
which afflicted the Israelites in the wilderness,
the image of one of which was lifted up by Moses;
and how far that serpentine figure was an emblem of the Divine Light shall be next considered.

¹ Numbers, xxi. 6th, 8th, and 9th verses.—
" And the Lord sent fiery serpents among the
" people. And the Lord said unto Moses, make
" thee a fiery serpent and set it upon a pole;
" and it shall come to pass, that every one that
" is bitten, when he looketh upon it, shall live.
" And Moses made a serpent of brass, &c."
The looking unto this figure was to give health
and salvation to the offending Israelites. And
we expect salvation only by " looking unto

" Jesus, the author and finisher of our faith,
" who, for the joy that was set before him,
" endured the cross." Heb. xii. 2. But let us
see what the ancient Jews, before our Saviour,
thought of it, and how Christ himself applied
it.

The opinion of the ancient Jews, may be
seen in the Wisdom of Solomon, xvi. 5, 6, 7.
" For when the horrible fierceness of beasts came
" upon these and they perished with the stings
" of crooked serpent, thy wrath endured not
" for ever. But they were troubled for a small
" season, that they might be admonished,
" having a sign of salvation to put them in
" remembrance of the commandment of thy
" law. For he that turned himself towards it,
" was not saved by the things that he saw,
" but by Thee that art the Saviour of All."—
Is not this the very sense and language of the
Apostle? They were not saved by looking up
unto the serpent, as such, but by looking up
unto Jesus (in that symbol) who endured the
cross.

John, iii. 14, 15.—" As Moses lifted up the
" serpent in the wilderness, even so must the
" Son of Man be lifted up ; that whosoever be-
" lieveth in Him should not perish, but have
" everlasting life." The words are of themselves
plain and decisive.

A very learned author is of opinion, that,
" in it, the presence, in the manner it was in
" the Cherubim, resided; because it cured all
" who were bitten by those serpents, and looked
" upon it, as the real presence does those who
" look at Christ upon the cross. Isaiah, chap.
" vi. makes use of this name with the same re-
" presentation as the Cherubim had ; which

" connects the Seraph, the emblem hung up in
" the wilderness, which cured those who were
" biten and would look at it, and the Seraph
" Christ, who, as all men have been bitten,
" cures every one who would look at Him upon
" the cross." Whatever may be thought of this
notion, (of the presence resident in the emblem)
'tis very probable, that the Israelites themselves
entertained the same: since we find them burning incense to it even in the days of Hezekiah.

As for the supposed impropriety of it on
account of the curse denounced against the serpent at the fall, it is sufficient to observe, that
" Christ redeemed us from the curse of the law,
" being made a curse for us ; for it is written,
" cursed is every one that hangeth on a tree."—
Galat. iii. 13.

But to take off every shadow of an objection
to the propriety of this symbol; be it remem-
bered once again, that it had no concern in the
fall of man ; that it is not of the same species
with that, of which it was said, " Upon thy
" belly shall thou go, and dust shalt thou eat
" all the days of thy life;" but the flaming or
fiery-flying serpent: and was therefore considered as a fit emblem of light and life: whereas,
the ancient emblem of death was, the creeping
serpent biting the heel of the woman.

As some well-meaning persons have con-
ceived a distaste for these pieces of antiquity,
and have pronounced them the remnants of idolatry and the dishonors of human nature; it be-
hoves us to pay this deference to the tender con-
science, and to obviate the prejudices of intem-
perate zeal. Upon the whole then, the reader
will consider, that the figures here delineated,
were emblems, not objects of worship; and

only answered the end of an inscription, before
the use of letters: that the stones, which formed
them, were but the constituent parts of a sacred
edifice ; and no man adores the temple, but the
divinity supposed to inhabit there. The most
bigoted Christian of any denomination, was
never yet accused of worshipping a church,
though erected in the figure of a cross.

## History of the Druids, &c.

The topographical and geographical part of the history of this globe, is so obscure beyond Noah and the flood, that it does not permit us to know any thing concerning this famous island, before these epochas; nor can we even conjecture whether or no it was inhabited at that time; though from the first chapter of Genesis, the world appears to have been extremely populous in its antediluvian ages.

It may rationally be concluded, from the various opinions of the best historians, that this island received its first inhabitants, from the eastern parts of the world, adjoining to the place where Noah and his family came to settle on the decrease of the waters. They seem to have proceeded, gradually as they increased, peopleing first a great part of Asia, as far as the mountain Taurus. At the extremity of this high mountain, in that neck of ground, called from thence, Taurica Chersonesus, the offspring of Magog settled, whence they were named Magogæi; Scythæ; then Cimmerii; afterwards, by contraction, Cimbri and Cumeri, because they lived there in a perpetual kind of winter.

These Cimbri, were a very valiant and warlike nation. Tully writes of them, that it was their delight to die in battle, and that nothing so much tormented them, as to be taken away idly in their beds. No wonder, therefore, if leaving Cœlosyria, their first seat, proceeding over the mountain Taurus, they conquered ~~many nations~~, and became possessors of almost the whole continent of Europe. Through several ~~circumstances of the places~~ they possessed, they were called Sachas, Germani, Celtæ, Galatæ, and Galli; and from these Cimbri, proceeded those called Cymri or Cumeri, who, in all probability, came first, to inhabit and people the north of this island, 7 or 800 years after the flood.

That the Gauls, a numerous nation of the continent, (on the opposite shores) went, not long after the Cumeri, to the southern parts of this island, is very probable; not only on account of a great similitude, found in the manners of the two nations, but a likeness in their form and complexion.

About 500 years before Christ, according to Siay, two large colonies were sent out of that country; the one to Italy; and the other to Germany, by Ambigalus, who then governed it; we may therefore suppose, that when Gaul was overstocked with people, they would not all ramble, or be sent, to countries at a distance, when Britain was so much nearer, and better known to them.

The Phœnicians, another nation of the remotest antiquity, living near the most eastern part of the Mediterranean sea, at Tyre and Sidon; who were a people of great knowledge, and traded in the primitive ages of the world, are supposed, by their advantage of shipping, and the many colonies they had upon the straits, to be contemporary with the Cimbri and Gauls, in this island.

From these Phœnicians, is to be deduced, the first antiquity of this nation, upon account of their voyages hither, which may be proved by the authority of the best authors.

They first reached this island, as may be gathered by ancient histories, before the Trojan war, and long before the first Olympiad, (the beginning of which, according to the Julian account, was anno 3938; from the year of the world, 3256; from the temple, &c. 263). Some say, it was their famous Hercules, others Himilco, who was sent with a fleet, through the straits, to discover the western seas.

The cause of making them so early mariners, was not only through their ambition for empire, and particular genius for navigation and merchandize, but through the necessity of inventing the best and safest way of escaping the hands of Joshua, who persecuted them with an army of Israelites; and after having made themselves masters of most part of the Land of Canaan, drove them into a nook of the earth, too small to contain so numerous a body; when they put themselves into shipping, to seek their fortunes in other parts of the world, of which company, Britain received a considerable share.

This skilful, trading people, finding these islands abounded with tin and lead mines, called them Barat-anac, or Bratanac, viz. a country of tin; and Alben, changed after, by the Greeks, into Albion; which is now called England.— They exported immense quantities of metals and skins, which they exchanged with the inhabitants for salt, earthen pots, and brazen ware. The parts of the country they more particularly traded with, were the west coast of Cornwall,

c

Devonshire, and the Scilly Islands, taking no notice of the northern parts. They esteemed the Bratanacs, (whence is derived Bretannica, Britannia, and then Britain) a very considerable part of the world, on account of the useful commodities they afforded them; and indeed they proved a mine of gold, in their hands.

The utility of those excellent commodities they exported from this country, through the Mediterranean Seas, to Greece, rendered the Greeks very curious after the search of it ; but the Phœnicians, to whom that trade had been a peculiar monopoly, disposing of lead and tin, to all other nations, at their own prices, were very careful not to let any other know this navigation.

They had great markets, particularly at Narbo, which they kept well provided, for the great extent of their trade by land, as well as to conceal this treasure from the world, being exceedingly jealous, least the source and head of their commerce should be discovered, and the busy Grecians receive the same benefit.— They very carefully and studiously concealed it for many years from the Greeks and Romans, who knew this country, only by report. Strabo, in the third book of his Geography, says, " That " a Roman vessel, having followed a Phœnician " merchant ship, that they might learn this " traffic of merchandize ; the Phœnician master, " from spiteful envy, ran his ship on purpose " upon the sands, whereby he brought the Roman, " who followed, into the same danger of de- " struction, himself escaping the wreck. He " afterwards received, out of the public trea- " sury, the worth of the commodities and wares " he had lost; which example was afterwards

" imitated by many others in the same occur-
" rences."

In process of time, the Phœnician state
declined, the trade was much neglected, and their
wars were unsuccessful; which obliged that long
fortunate people to give up their commerce and
intercourse with this nation. The Athenians
now took advantage of this, for, being at
war with the Persians, whom they completely
defeated by sea, compelled them to take refuge
in the river Hurymedom, in Pamphylia; they
then dispatched their great Admiral Cimon, son
of the brave Miltiades, with a considerable
number of gallies, well manned, to attack their
fleet, which he soon reached and overcame,
taking some and sinking others: on the same
day, meeting accidentally with a fleet of Phœnicians, coming to the aid of the Persians, with
whom they were allied, he seized upon their
navy, forsaken by the owners almost before he
could prepare for battle: and thus were the
Grecians peaceably left masters of the seas,
without any copartners in the profit and glory.

Having now the most expert and able
seamen, and exceeding every other nation in the
number of her shipping, it will not be irrational
to conclude from the following reasons: That,
availing themselves of so many advantages, with
so favourable an opportunity, and having heard
of the Bratannacs, now learnt the way to them,
and came to Britain to trade with them: 1st,
from their measuring all their actions by profit,
undertaking any voyage, however long and te-
dious, if they could promise themselves to be
well recompenced for their labor and hazard.—
2nd, Their ambitious endeavours in getting into
their hands all the islands they could; witness

those in the Grecian Seas; and their adventuring such infinite losses, such as the ruin of their whole fleet, rather than quit their pretensions to Sicily, in no respect to be compared to this our island; which besides, they had long coveted, and been in search of.—3rd, Because there is no doubt, but some false and cowardly renegado Phœnician, who had formerly traded hither, discovered to them the situation and fertility of this island, in the same manner as the renegado Greek, shewed the Persians a way over a ridge of mountains, whereby the Lacedæmonians were encompassed, at the straits of Thermopylæ; which otherwise, in all probability they had never found out; neither could they long be ignorant of the Phœnicians transporting their commodities of tin and lead from this island.—4th, They were also likely to understand the value of this island, from the Phoceans, an Athenian colony; who, dreading the Persian tyranny, set sail with their families, and landed in France, where they founded Marseilles, and, in all probability, learnt all the particulars of this island.

The places were the Greeks first landed, are generally thought to be the two islands Man and Anglesey; where are found most of the Grecian remains. They contented themselves with the commodities of the southern and western countries, until they had gradually accustomed themselves to the nature of the people, and conveniencies of situations. They did not venture too far northward, so that Scotland was very little, if at all known to them.

We may judge how far they extended themselves over the continent; as Julius Cæsar says, their language, religion, &c. were rooted even in the barren mountains, inhabited by the Helvetii. This people, weary of their country, burnt their houses, and agreed upon a general march of the whole nation, to seek some new plantations. The first difficulty they had to encounter was, to get out, securely bounded as they were with hills and rivers, that it seemed to them rather a prison than a defence; and being afterwards beaten by Cæsar and compelled to return, they brought to him table-books, written in Greek letters, recording the number of all that went forth, how many bore arms, besides old women and children.

This is an evident proof of the footing the Greeks had in these parts, the work of several centuries; many are of opinion, that they were the first planters in this island; though it is certain they succeeded the Phoenicians.

It is not a little surprizing, that learned and active as they were, and inhabiting this island for several centuries, that they never discovered it to be an island; even in Julius Cæsar's time, Britain was only supposed to be one, and was not really known so, till Agricola's fleet sailed round it.

The Britons and Gauls having properly but one and the same religion, resorted hither to public seminaries, wishing to be better instructed in the learning and religion of the Druids, who went over every year, to assist at the religious ceremonies of the Gauls.

The Druids must have been here very early, since persons of indisputable learning, have thought them to be of British origin. But this opinion has been refuted, and the contrary ascertained by men of too transcendent merit and talents to be disputed. Dr. STUKELY says, they first made their appearance from the eastern parts of the world, about the time of Abraham. Their name bespeaks them of Greek extraction, although they were known here before the Greeks, but as it seems clearly denoted by their doctrine and religious customs, we are inclined to think they were Cimbri, Phœnicians, or Idumeans. The Cimbri, who called themselves the sons of Hercules, were wont to sacrifice men, particularly strangers, who fell into their hands.

As in the British History there are many things altogether impossible, others very improbable and fabulous; yet, as there may be many truths couched under the whole, we think it necessary to give a full account of this particular part of our history, partly upon that very reason, and partly because many judicious authors do not deny them.

The ancient Druids were generally thought to be the second Order known in Britain and Gaul; but it is necessary we should speak of the first, from which they were derived.

The most ancient Order of people in Britain, is that of the Bardi, though in time the Druids obtained a superiority over them, in point of esteem. The Bardi were, (according to STRABO) poets and songsters; singing in recitative music, the praises of great men. Others say, they derived their name and origin from Bardus, called the King of the Celts, son of Druis, one of the most ancient kings of the Gauls, from whom they also pretend the Druids to have been named.

These Bardi or Bards were, no doubt, at first of a religious order, and employed themselves in deifying great men, composing verses

and singing them, while playing upon their
Nablium or Cynira; also in praise of heroes, at
their apotheosis, which in ancient times was
not only esteemed glorious for the dead, and
useful to the living, but also a religious and acceptable act to the Gods.

This custom originated in the east, where
it was practised from the earliest period. It
was communicated to the Greeks, and afterwards to the Latins. The ancient Greeks had
not only the whole body of their Divinity in
verse, but upon all occasions, as marriages,
funerals, &c. their religious rites and ceremonies were performed in it; likewise upon
occasion of some great deliverance or remarkable victory, they sang the praises of
their gods, composing odes and hymns, which
they rehearsed to the people, in a solemn manner, with music.

The Bards were also very much given to
composing genealogies, and rehearsing them in
public assemblies, in which they were very
skilful. The profession of a Bard required more
that ordinary abilities; and were the priests of
those days. HOMER mentions Demodocus and
Veisses, as celebrated Bards.

The Bards, who hitherto were the only religious Order, and whose compositions were
used in the most solemn rites, degenerated
by degrees, into the nature of common ballad-
makers, and from singing of the essence and immortality of the soul, the works of nature, the
course of cœlestial bodies, the order and harmony
of the spheres, the praises of the Gods, and
rehearsing the virtues and actions of great
men; which was considered necessary in order
to stimulate and encourage the people to great

enterprises; became the divulgers of idle and empty genealogies, more for gain than the advancement of virtue, and afterwards gave themselves up to composing mystical rhymes, abounding with prophecies of things to come; to charms, spells, incantations, the art of magic and necromancy; insomuch that they had sundry verses to that purpose, which were considered of wonderful power and energy.

Long was Britain sorely infested with them, notwithstanding they were superseded by the Evates or Eubates, another branch of philosophers and priests, who continued to practise and preach morality and virtue, until they gave place to the Druids, who were far more numerous.

The name of the Druids, proceeded from the Greek word Drus, or Druades, an oak, and was given to them, from the oaks that grew in the plain of Mamre, in the valley of Hebron, under which, in the earliest times, those religious men, to whom the office of priesthood was committed, lived most devoutly. We read in Genesis, that Abraham pitched his tent and dwelt among the oaks of Mamre, that he built a tabernacle and altar unto the Lord, in which he offered rams, goats, calves, &c. in sacrifice; and moreover, that he performed there all other sacerdotal rites and ceremonies appertaining to his priestly office; and the Lord appeared unto him. Abraham is also said, to have planted a grove in Beersheba, and to have invoked there the name of Jehovah: this grove was of oak.— And Abraham passed through the Land unto the place of Sichem, unto the oak or oak grove, of Moreh. And he built there an altar unto the Lord who appeared unto him. Moses afterwards distinguished the place by the Oaks of Moreh.—It is said of Jacob, that being about to make a solemn dedication, of himself and his household, to the service of God, and having received of them all the strange Gods that were in their hands, and all the ear-rings that were in their ears, he hid them under the oak, or oak grove, which was by Shechem. So the men of Shechem and the house of Millo, made Abimelech King by the oak grove of the pillar, that was by Shechem: translated in the margin of our bibles, the Oak of the Pillar. The Hebrew word Alah, which signifies an oath, signifies also the oak tree; which was therefore held in great veneration, and esteemed a sacred emblem of that covenant, in which the divine confederators had mutually engaged themselves, for the redemption of mankind: a tree, which, for this reason, was especially reverenced at one time or other by all nations.

Under the Oaks of Mamre, sprang the original sect of Druids, and it is positively recorded by some authors, that the Druid colleges flourished very eminently in the days of Hermio, a German prince, which happened not long after Abraham's death. This very much tends to prove the antiquity of that sect; and by reason that Abraham lived under these oaks so piously. The Druids, wishing to imitate his example, though degenerating from the true substance and intent of so good an example, chose groves of oaks, under which they performed all invented rites and ceremonies belonging to their religion.

According to Julius Cæsar's account, the Druidical institution first took rise in Britain, and passed thence into Gaul; but his opinion

was never well established, and very often con-
tradicted; but be that as it may, the argument
serves to prove, that the Druids were the second
order of people in this island.

Sarron, third king of the Britons and Celts,
is feigned to be the founder of the Sarronides,
which was merely another name for the Druids.

In a certain monastery, upon the confines
of Vaitland, in Germany, were found six old
statues, which being exposed to view, Conradus
Celtes, who was then present, was of opinion,
they were the figures of ancient Druids. They
were seven feet in height, bare footed, and their
heads covered with a Greekish hood, with a
scrip by their sides, and a beard descending from
their nostrils, plated out in two divisions, to
their middle; in their hands was a book and a
Diogenes staff, five feet in length; their coun-
tenances were severe and morose, and their eyes
directed to the earth.—They were placed at the
gates of the temple.

It is supposed that the Greek language, or
a dialect thereof, was preserved entire only
among the Druids, who received it from some
plantation of the people in these parts; what
makes us more confident in our judgment is,
that the Druids had the very same interest, and
used the same practice as the Roman clergy did,
in adhering to the ancient Latin tongue. The
Roman clergy took notice of a great jealousy in
the Druids, lest their learning and religion
should be understood and divulged; so much
so, that it was accounted unlawful to reveal
any of their mysteries.

Their public records were preserved in
characters of the Greek tongue, which being
unintelligible by the vulgar, none could have

recourse to them, but persons of repute and
learning. Nothing was permitted to be taken
away in writing; and a trust was reposed in
some particular persons, who by their singular
integrity and long experience of fidelity and
learning, were chosen for that purpose.

They committed nothing to public writing.
Pisistratus was the first person that exposed to
public view, books of the liberal arts and sciences
at Athens; and the way of composing in numbers was left off in Greece a little before the
day of Herodotus, who, notwithstanding, en-
titled his books by the names of the Muses.

The first establishment of christian religion,
by public authority, is very early, being 181
years after the death of Christ. The reason
why it was so early known in Britain, above
other nations, was because of the learning, piety,
and devotion of the Druids; for many of the
tenets, of which the immortality of the soul
was the chief, were great inlets to their religion,
which, besides the great virtue and holiness it
carried with it, taught rewards of virtue and
punishments of vice, upon safer grounds than
the Heathens had ever built for their imaginary
virtue: namely, evident miracles, and certain
demonstrations, that there was an Almighty
power, who strictly examined the actions of
every man.

The religion of the Druids flourished a long
time, both in Britain and Gaul. It spread as
far as Italy, as appears by Augustus's injunc-
tion to the Romans, not to celebrate its mysteries. There were female as well as male Druids.
It was a female Druid of Tungria, (the late
bishopric of Liege, in the Netherlands) that
foretold to Dioclesian, (when a private soldier
in Gallia) that he would be Emperor of Rome.

Britain was divided into several petty governments, as to civil affairs; Kent alone having four distinct kingdoms within it; the government of the Druids was universal over the whole island, and some part of Gallia also; so that their power and interest was infinitely the greater, being subject only to two Primates; whereof one presided over the North Druids, the other over the South. The former of which is supposed to have his residence in the Isle of Man; the latter in Anglesey; although it is thought by some, there was but one chief: so that, though the secular power might often clash, by reason of its many decisions, by being divided in many kingdoms, the interest and authority of the Druids was preserved entire, by their unity under one head, to whom, once a year, they had recourse in public meetings and assemblies; which custom they received from the Bardi, who had it from the Phœnicians; for in the eastern nations, as India, Egypt, and Syria, we find that the power of the priest was in a manner distinct from the civil government, and the calling of assemblies and general meetings was absolutely in their power, and independent of the temporal magistrate; which custom, nevertheless, in those days, was often abridged, by wise and politic princes.

The primate of these Druid Priests, was a sort of Pontiff, constituted by election; and being a place of eminent repute and authority, its vacancy caused many candidates; so much so, that whenever the secular power was engaged in the contest, every prince endeavoured to oblige his favorite, and to strengthen his authority. Sometimes when the candidates were of equal merit, such heats and broils have raged among them, that blows have ensued before the election was over.

The Druids were held in such veneration by the people, that their authority was almost absolute. No public affairs were transacted without their approbation; not so much as a malefactor could be put to death without their consent. Religion not only afforded them a pretence to interfere in the government, but authorized them, as they pretended, to intermeddle in private affairs. Under pretence that there could not be any case but where religion might be concerned, they claimed a power of excommunication, which was the greatest punishment that could be inflicted, and by which means they became very formidable. These excommunications were much after the manner of ours; for by them, such as refused to submit to the determinations of the Druids, were excluded from the sacrifices; and a person so interdicted, was declared one of the number of the profani, that is, wicked wretches; nay, he was deemed so infamous, that all persons studiously avoided him, not daring to approach him, or converse, though at a distance, for fear of being infected with so dangerous a curse. They were rendered incapable of any honorable office, and entirely excluded from the law, as to their estates.

They had other ways of punishing the contemners of their religion; and had considerable rewards for the obedient.

They were made judges of all controversies, both private and public; such as murder, manslaughter, theft, &c. or if suits arose about inheritance, or strife concerning the boundary of lands; they gave absolute judgment: and did not execute their decrees by the temporal authority, but issued their excommunications upon the non-performance of them; which, as they were of all punishments the most grievous, so were they inflicted not only upon private but public persons; and, no doubt, extended to their magistrates and governors.

To them was committed the care of providing sacrifices; of prescribing laws for their worship; they were the sole interpreters of religion, in the exercise of which their presence was absolutely necessary; they proclaimed public sacrifices as they saw occasion; and no private ones could be performed without them.

Some of their Maxims may serve as a specimen of their principles and religion, which were with great difficulty collected by a learned Turgundian author; of which the following are the most remarkable:—

None must be instructed but in the sacred groves.

Misletoe must be gathered with reverence; and if possible, in the sixth moon.—It must be cut with a golden bill.

Every thing derived its origin from heaven.

The Arcana of the sciences must not be committed to writing, but to the memory.

Great care is to be taken in the education of children.

The powder of misletoe makes women fruitful.

The disobedient are to be shut out from the sacrifices.

Souls are immortal.

The soul after death goes into other bodies.

If the world is destroyed, it will be by fire or water.

Upon extraordinary emergencies a man must be sacrificed.

According as the body falls, or moves after it is fallen; according as the blood flows, or the wound opens, future events are foretold.

Prisoners of war are to be slain upon the altars, or burnt alive enclosed in wicker, in honor of their gods.

All commerce with strangers must be prohibited.

He that comes last to the assembly of the states, ought to be punished with death.

Children are to be brought up apart from their parents, till they are fourteen years of age.

Money lent in this world, will be repaid in the next.

There is another world, and they who kill themselves to accompany their friends thither, will live with them there.

Letters given to dying persons, or thrown upon the funeral piles of the dead, will be faithfully delivered in the other world.

The moon is a sovereign remedy for all things, (as its name in Celtic implies.)

Let the disobedient be excommunicated; let him be deprived of the benefit of the law; let him be avoided by all, and rendered incapable of any employ.

All masters of families are kings in their own houses; they have a power of life and death over their wives, children, and slaves.

They sacrificed men as well as beasts, who were generally enemies or malefactors, but sometimes innocent natives; for which cause, they were very much feared and reverenced by the people. They had the power of determining what person was fittest for that purpose, and whose blood would be most acceptable to the gods.

The Druids were exempted from the services of war, and paid no taxes as the people did; by which immunities many were invited, on their own free wills, to enter into that order and discipline; and many were sent by their friends and relations to learn it.— It was taught in Gaul, as well as Britain, yet not so perfectly as in the Isles of Man and Anglesey.

Mona, or Anglesey, at that time, was very populous, from the concourse of people that fled thither for security, and a place of no small annoyance to the Romans. To invade it, Cæsar first built flat-bottomed boats to carry over his infantry; the cavalry followed either upon the flats and shallows, or where it was deeper swam it. Upon the shore stood, ready to receive them, a strange medley of an army, composed of men, women, and priests; the men were well armed, but the women and priests ran about like furies, the former with their hair in confusion, and in black garments; and the latter carrying torches before them, with their hands lifted up to heaven, pouring forth direful execrations. The Romans, at first, were astonished at such a sight, but animating each other not to fear such an army of mad-women and lunatics, bore on the standards, and trampled down all before them: they then placed garrisons on the conquered, and cut down the groves consecrated to their superstition.

After the conquest of Anglesey, the remainder of them fled into Britain as their last refuge, and remained here until King Cratilinth, (An. Dom. 277) with great difficulty drove them out.

The next seat of the Druids (after their retreat from Anglesey) we have every reason to believe was Great Barr, situated a little south of Sutton Coldfield, on the fine eminence, called Barr Beacon, which stretches itself out like a great barrier to the country beyond. Dr. Wilkes says, "Barr may either be derived from "the Hebrew word Bara, a wild uncultivated "field; or Barah, to eat, refresh themselves; "or from the Saxon word Bearew, a grove or "little wood;" such a one, in all probability, being here kept for their use: and according to Pliny, "nothing could be better adapted, than "that part of the hill, called Barr Beacon, to "their observations of the heavenly bodies." The Druids always gave notice of the quarterly days of sacrifice, by fires made on the high hills; and none, in these parts, are more eligible than this for that purpose : and for the same reason it afterwards was thought a proper place to alarm this part of the kingdom, by a beacon which was placed here, whenever the Danes came to plunder this part of the country.

At the declivity of very pleasingly diversified hills, near Quieslade, is a most delightful lake, by crossing the head of which, the admirer of variegated landscape will be amply rewarded by an agreeable range over the opposite hills, where the High-Wood and Barr Beacon present themselves to view ; and by gradually climbing the first of these two summits, the south-east prospect becomes very rich and extensive ; and the latter presents an unbounded panorama into fifteen counties, which PLOT, in his History of Staffordshire, has specified. The Druids having very wisely chosen this for an observatory, it was afterwards made the site of a beacon during the savage contests between the Saxons and Danes ; which spot has been recently devoted to other serious and philosophic purposes.

The county of Stafford lies undoubtedly about the middle of this island : formerly it was nearly covered with wood, and at this day we have three very large forests, besides many lesser commons, once covered in like manner ; so that perhaps a third part of it lies uncultivated. Sutton-Coldfield was once a part of the forest of Cank or Cannock, and perhaps there was none more extensive at that time in the whole kingdom.

The word Cannock, which is nothing more than a translation of the British name of this forest into the Saxon language, had its original derived from the religious ceremonies performed by the Druids in this great wood or forest : the word Coldfield most probably signifying the field or habitation of the religious, like Cannock; and many others in the neighbourhood had relation to the religious ceremonies performed by the Druids thereabout. On the west side of Sutton-Coldfield runs a very high hill, almost directly north and south. At the north end lies the village of Aldridge, and the south end is Barr, a village belonging to it. Under this hill, on the north-east side, arise many springs, which run into one body called Bowen-pool : hence a brook of the same name runs by Aston and Shenstone to Hints and Tamworth ; there joins the Trent, and runs direct to Hull. Near Aldridge, a small common, to this day, retains the name of Druid-heath ; and near to the pool, at the east end, is a small area or parcel of ground, about 80 yards by 30, encompassed with a treble ditch. This being much too small for a great number of men, or an army, must therefore have been the seat of some public or private family. About two or three hundred yards towards the south is a hill exactly round, encompassed with a single ditch, and rising from the level of the ground about 7 or 8 feet : the diameter is about 6 yards. It has never been ploughed ; but what the use of it may have been was never determined. We suppose that it was the summer seat of the Arch-Druid, for the reasons above given : and about two miles to the north of it, adjoining to the old Roman road called Streetway, is another area much of the same size, encompassed likewise with a treble ditch. Here the situation is loftier and drier, so that he might possibly make this his place of residence in the winter. It is now called Knave's Castle, as if some robber had here secreted himself to plunder travellers, since the times of the Britons.

Nothing could be better adapted than Barr Beacon to the observations made by the Druids on the heavenly bodies. The prospect from it is perhaps as beautiful as from any part of England: here we view great part of Warwickshire, Leicestershire, Derbyshire, Staffordshire, Cheshire, Shropshire, Worcestershire, and several counties in Wales. Near Barr, one part of it is known by the name of Barr Beacon, where now grows a clump of trees, that serve as a landmark, and help to please the weary traveller.

Neither the Greeks nor Romans ever used a treble ditch on any occasion: both these people were fond of the number three, as being the next odd number to unity. Pythagoras is said to have brought this reverence for odd numbers out of Egypt; and in all probability this doctrine came originally from the children of Israel during their captivity there, if the word Elohim does really comprehend the idea of a Trinity, as some have lately endeavoured to demonstrate. As our Druids undoubtedly came originally from the East, and committed nothing to writing, they might emblematically make such ditches about the seat of their high-priest; for Diogenes, Gaertius, and others, assure us, that they taught philosophy obscurely or enigmatically by symbols. If then, for the reasons here given, we allow these to have been the habitations of the Arch-Druid, they must have been made long before the time of Julius Cæsar, while they had a notion of the Trinity; because he tells us, that in his time they taught the people to worship more gods than one, and soon after became idolators.

Many temples of the Druids are said to be yet in part remaining in this island and that of Anglesey. Dr. STUKELEY will have them to be all built by the Jewish cubit, which the Phœ-cians first brought hither; and many of them were made of extraordinary large stones, as at Abery and Stonehenge; others were made of timber, and, as may be supposed, have long ago been destroyed by age and other accidents. Their altars were sometimes made of one and sometimes of three stones. In this country we often find very large stones by themselves, where-of the better sort of mill-stones are made; but whether any of those about Cannock were ever British deities, as Dr. PLOT asserts, or ever served as the crom-lech or altar, cannot be af-firmed with certainty.

In this and other parts of the kingdom a kind of brazen instrument has frequently been found, about six inches long, three broad, at the larger end, and in shape not unlike a mason's lath hammer, except their being taken down to an edge at both ends; there is a sort of groove at the lesser end, and a partition in the middle; and some have a ring or loop-hole in one side. Dr. PLOT imagines they might have been the Ro-man Securis or axe, or their Catapula; and Mr. Borlase calls them Celts. To me they seem to be British; for from their shape they could cut only upwards, when fixed at the end of a pole or staff. The Druids or their servants might prune away the superfluous branches of the misletoe with such an instrument. The loop-hole served to fix it by a string to their girdle; and if their walking-staff was at the upper end fitted to re-ceive the lesser end of the tool, there would not be much trouble in joining them together;

and by forcing it upwards, or striking the lower
end of the staff with any thing hard, there would
be little difficulty in cutting off a small branch
of oak or misletoe. The Arch-Druid is said to
have cut the misletoe on solemn days with an
instrument of gold, which is now generally
drawn as a crooked knife or hook; but who can
tell whether it was not of the form here described?

The strict life of the Druids in these two
islands, had rendered them both more valuable
than others, upon all the accounts aforesaid:
here they were sequestered from the cares of the
world; men of upright and moral conversation;
here also were their general meetings; here they
taught and discoursed of nothing but virtue and
piety. Their solemn assemblies were all concerning the principles of divinity, morality, the
immortality of the soul, and the world to come;
the study of astronomy and philosophy, as well
as that of natural religion; the perfect education of young men; and those who had not been
instructed by them, were not esteemed sufficiently qualified to manage the affairs of state.

As priests, they had of course the care and
direction of all religious matters:

> The Druids, now, while arms are heard no more,
> Old mysteries and barb'rous rights restore:
> A tribe who singular religion love,
> And haunt the lonely coverts of the grove.
> To these, and these of all mankind alone,
> The gods are sure reveal'd or sure unknown.
> If dying mortals' doom they sing aright,
> No ghosts descend to dwell in dreadful night:
> No parting souls to grisly Pluto go,
> Nor seek the dreary silent shades below:
> But forth they fly immortal in their kind,
> And other bodies in new worlds they find.

Thus life for ever runs its endless race,
And like a line, death but divides the space;
A stop which can but for a moment last,
A point between the future and the past.
Thrice happy they beneath their northern skies,
Who, that worst fear, the fear of death despise:
Hence they no cares for this frail being feel,
But rush undaunted on the pointed steel;
Provoke approaching fate, and bravely scorn
To spare that life which must so soon return.

LUCAN.

They not only performed their rites and
ceremonies upon hills and in groves, but inhabited them, as before said, by preference; for
which purpose they planted many in this island.
These groves were inclosements of spreading
oaks, surrounding their sacred places of worship,
which they called *ghwm*, hence probably the
word *glen*, signifying now in Welsh a church, and
in which were *gorseddan*, or hillocks, where they
sat and pronounced their decrees, and harangued
the people; *cornedde*, or heaps of stones, on
which they had a peculiar mode of worship;
and *cromleche*, or altars, on which they performed the solemnities of sacrifices. So great was
their estimation for oak, that no divine service
could be performed but under the shades of
oaken groves: they could not perform any sacrifice without a branch of it; and they paid the
most sacred reverence to all they found growing
to it, particularly misletoe, which they worshipped as a thing sent unto them by Heaven, considering it as their greatest blessing: so when they
found misletoe upon an oak, they accounted it a
sure sign the god they served had chosen that tree
and spot where it grew, as a particular place he
was pleased to be adored at. All these customs
are so connected with those of the eastern nations, that we may surely believe they originated

from the Cimbri, Phœnicians, and Greeks. If
we consider besides, that Moses found great difficulty in keeping the Children of Israel, on their
return from Egypt, from doing the same, notwithstanding they were told it was highly dis-
pleasing to the Almighty. All the idolatrous
worship of the heathens had its origin from
thence; and the oak was ever esteemed the king
of trees, and in all ages greatly reverenced, and
called sacred.

They gathered misletoe with many super-
stitious ceremonies and great devotion, cutting
it down with a golden bill. At the end of the
year they generally went in search of it, with
great reverence, gathering branches and leaves
of it, which they offered to Jupiter, inviting all
people to the ceremony by these words, which
they caused to be proclaimed, " *Come to the oak
branches of the new year.*"

In the particular gathering of misletoe they
principally observed that the moon was six days
old; for on that day they began their months
and new years, and their several ages had their
revolution every thirtieth year.

In the next place, having prepared their
sacrifices and feasts under an oak where misletoe
grew, they brought two young bullocks, milk
white, whose horns had never before been bound;
and the priest, being clothed in a white vesture,
climbed the tree, and, having a bill of gold in
his hand, cut off the misletoe, which those below
received in a white cassock; then they offered
the sacrifice, and blessed the gift, by mumbling
over many orations, that it might be prosperous
to the receivers; all which ceremonies duly performed, it was esteemed a sovereign antidote

against all poison, and a certain remedy against barrenness, both in men, women, and beasts.

They had a herb called Samolus, viz. marsh-wort, or fen-berries, which, as its name implies in English, grew in wet places; in gathering which they used ceremonies: first, they were fasting—secondly, they ought not to look back during the time of their plucking it—and, lastly, they were to use their left hand only.

PLINY, who mentions this herb, does not tell us what it was; but it seems very probable, that, from the last ceremony, namely, gathering it with the left hand, the herb took its name, that is to say, Samol, signifying in the Phœnician tongue the left hand. This herb, so gathered, was esteemed of sovereign virtue in the cure of all diseases in swine or other cattle.

The high antiquity and universality of sacrifices, bespeak it originally a divine institution. There is great probability that the clothing of our first parents consisted of the skins of beasts sacrificed by Adam in the interval between his offence and expulsion from Paradise.

Of this most solemn act of religion we find, from the practice of the Patriarchs, that penitence and purification were necessary attendants: nor was an invocation in the name Jehovah, the great propitiator, at this time wanting.

The practice of these public offices of religion includes the observance of one day in seven, made holy by the Creator from the beginning; the use of altars, and the early foundation of temples.

Accordingly, we read that Noah (by whom the true worship was preserved) immediately after the flood, built an altar unto Jehovah, and

took of every clean beast, and of every clean
fowl, and offered burnt-offerings on the altar.
So Abraham built an altar unto Jehovah, who
appeared unto him. Again, the same Father of
the Faithful built an altar unto Jehovah, and
invoked in the name Jehovah. So likewise,
Isaac built an altar, and invoked in the name
Jehovah.

Where these altars were placed there was
said to be, in those early ages of the world, a
house or temple of Jehovah, which were mostly
upon eminences, and always uncovered ; and,
where they could be had, upright stones were
erected near them. This in scripture is called,
*setting up a pillar:* nor was it done without a
particular form of consecration, of which the
behaviour of Jacob will explain the whole.

" And Jacob rose up early in the morning,
" and took the stone that he had put for his pil-
" low, and set it up for a pillar, and poured oil
" upon the top of it. And he called the name
" of that place Bethel, or the House of God.
" And Jacob vowed a vow, saying, if God will
" be with me, and will keep me in this way that
" I go, and will give me bread to eat and rai-
" ment to put on, so that I come again to my
" father's house in peace, then shall the Lord be
" my God. And this stone, which I have set up
" for a pillar, shall be God's house : and of all
" that thou shalt give me, I will surely give the
" tenth unto thee." In consequence of this,
he " built there an altar, and called the place
" El-beth-El ; and set up a pillar in the place
" where God talked with him, even a pillar of
" stone ; and he poured a drink-offering thereon,
" and he poured oil thereon. And Jacob called
" the name of the place Bethel." Here was a

temple with consecration and endowment; to which undoubtedly were made many additions, as it became very famous: for hence was the name Bethylia given afterwards to such like temples.

So likewise we are told that Moses rose up early in the morning, and built an altar under the hill, and twelve pillars.

At other times the altars were inclosed by groves of trees. Thus Abraham is said to have planted a grove in Beersheba, and to have invoked there in the name Jehovah.

As the Divine Presence, inhabiting the Cherubim on the east of Paradise, was signified by that irradiation of glory, which in our translation is called *a flaming sword turning every way*, and which directed mankind in the first ages to the place and object of religious worship; so these groves and stones were made to surround the altars in circular order, as best expressive of the same irradiation, and distinguishing such places as set apart for the public worship of the same God, who was supposed also to be there especially present; and whose infinity was likewise by the same figure acknowledged and intended. But where this symbol, expressive of the Divinity, was complex, then the circle was particularly applied to distinguish the person of the Father, being the figure of the solar body, which was considered as his great natural emblem.

For the patriarchal religion was not confined to the Patriarchs and their descendants, though it was preserved pure through them, while most of the nations fell into great corruptions; nor to the land of Canaan, in which they chiefly resided. Great part of Asia, Africa, the Continent of Europe, and the British Isles, were no strangers to the same doctrine, and abound with monuments of the same worship.

Al Janabius observes, that many of the Arabian idols were no other than large rude stones, the worship of which the posterity of Ishmael first introduced. To us it seems most probable, that these great stones were the first public places of divine worship amongst the Arabs, on which they poured wine and oil, as Jacob did upon the stones that served him for a pillow, when he saw his vision. Afterwards they might worship these stones themselves, as the Phoenicians in all probability did. Certain it is, that in process of time they were in most places desecrated by idolatry. The degenerate Canaanites particularly had, before the arrival of the Israelites in their country after the Exodus from Egypt, introduced into them the worship of graven images. For this reason God commanded his people, when they should enter into that land, to destroy their altars, break their pillars, cut down their groves, and burn their graven images with fire : and was then pleased to ordain a covered tabernacle for his peculiar worship ; a tabernacle covered with the skins of the sacrifices, and emblematical of Him who was one day to be covered with the infirmities of human flesh, and offered up for the sins of mankind.

The tomb of Zebulon, in Phoenicia, as it is called by travellers, consisting of two pillars at the distance of ten feet from each other, can be only two of these anointed or consecrated pillars.

" Mellcarthus, or the Tyrian Hercules, is said to have ordered Tyre to be built where the Petræ Ambrosiæ stood, which were two movea-

ble rocks standing by an olive tree. He was to
sacrifice on them, and they were to become fixed
and stable; that the city might be built with
happy auspices, and become permanent.

These Petræ Ambrosiæ (made moveable by
contrivance) were no other than stones consecrated or anointed with oil. Hence ambres are
anointed stones. They were the original patriarchal altars for libations and sacrifices, and
mean in general their altars, whether moveable
or immoveable; or as we may speak, their temples, which imply an altar properly inclosed with
stones and a ditch; or ground dedicated and set
apart for public celebration of religious rites.

We see it has been the custom, in the first
ages of the world, for all nations to immolate
living creatures unto their gods; even human
blood they shed upon their altars; nay, much
more, their own relatives, fathers, and mothers,
the new-born fruits of their accidental connec-
tions, and those too after the times of lawful
matrimony, they offered their imaginary propi-
tious or unfavourable gods. Concerning the
Jews, we find several testimonies in the sacred
Scriptures; and concerning other people, in a
great many ancient authors. This custom, tho'
altered more or less according to the different
progresses the various nations made in their civilization, was never entirely extirpated; some
people at this day uniting the benefit of some
polite arts and sciences with the barbarous
usages much like, if not the same as, the sacrificing of human creatures.

The first generations of men had neither
temples, nor statues for their gods, but worshipped towards the eastern heavens in the open air,

and sacrificed upon the summits of the highest mountains. This same custom is also attested in innumerable places of the sacred Scriptures: Abraham was commanded by God to offer Isaac his son for a burnt-offering upon one of the mountains in the land of Moriah. In later ages, when temples were used, they were often built upon the summits of mountains; very high mountains being commonly held sacred to Saturn or Jupiter, and sometimes to Apollo. But, as it has been before mentioned, groves of trees, woods, and shady places, were most looked for, preferred, and reverenced; nay, it was so common to erect altars and temples in groves, and to dedicate them to religious uses, that all sacred places, even those where no trees were, were called groves.

It seems to have been a custom, which prevailed not only in Europe, but over all the eastern countries, to attribute a sort of religion to groves; hence, among other precepts, whereby the Jews were kept from the imitation of the pagan religion, this was one: " *thou shalt not plant thee a grove of any trees near unto the altar of the Lord thy God.*" Several causes are assigned why groves came into so general request. As, first, the pleasantness of such places was apt to allure the people, and to beget in them a love for the religious worship paid there; especially in hot countries, where nothing is more delightful and refreshing than cool shades; for which cause the sacred groves consisted of tall and beautiful trees, rather than such as yielded fruit.

Secondly, The solitude of groves was thought very fit to create a religious awe and reverence in the minds of the people. Thus we are told by PLINY, that, in groves, the very silence of the place becomes the object of our adoration. SE-NECA also observes, that when we come into such places, the height of the trees, the solitude and secrecy of the place, and the horror which the shades impress upon us, possesses us with an opinion that some deity inhabits there.

Thirdly, Some are of opinion that groves derived their religion from the primitive ages of men, who lived in such places before the building of houses; and who had no other defence for their infants against wild beasts, or the weather, than what was afforded by boughs of trees compacted together; which was derived from Paradise, the seat of the first parents of mankind.

Groves held as the peculiar residence of the deity, were ornamented with a variety of offerings, excluding almost entirely the light of the sun; which were deemed most sacred, and as such carefully preserved pure and uninjured; sacrilege being punished with horrid, protracted torments, ending in death.

The Druids had all these customs among them still more refined, and no less cruel; and, indeed, death must have been looked upon by them as very little pain, since they used to inflict that punishment upon him who, in their general assemblies, came the last, to oblige the rest to be more attentive.

They held an opinion, that the life of a man, either in a desperate sickness, or in danger of war, could not be secured unless another suffered in his stead; so that in such cases they either offered men in sacrifice, or vowed so to do after their delivery; which vows they were obliged to perform.

*The Wicker Image.*

The most acceptable sacrifice to their gods they esteemed murderers, thieves, and robbers, and other heinous and notorious malefactors and criminals; but for want of these, innocent natives often suffered.

The most solemn sacrifice, either in Gaul or Britain, was the human hecatomb they offered under the shape of a man. They used to rear and dress up a huge statue, or image of a man, whose limbs consisted of twigs woven together in the nature of basket-ware: they filled it with live men, and after that, set it on fire, and so destroyed the poor creatures in the smoke and flames:—the strangeness of which custom we here represent.

This ceremony of sacrificing men to their idols in a wicker image, strange as it was, was not begun by chance, but upon some great occasion; and something extraordinary appears in the magnitude of the statue itself: they might do it in remembrance of Jupiter's victories over the titans and giants.

They are reported as employing sometimes beasts to fill it up when criminals were wanting, and to have taken innocent persons, in scarcity, though for the most part, convicts and captives in war used to be reserved for five years, and on a certain occasion burnt all together.

But they were so very cruel, that almost every week they not only murdered a great many upon their altars, but in their schools: Herphilus, one of their first doctors, taught anatomy over the bodies of living men at times to the number of seven hundreds.

Most certainly all these customs were derived from the heathens, whose festival fires were usually attended with the sacrifices of beasts,

but very often of men ; and this represented
the occasion of the solemnity ; a custom not left
off at this day, as sometimes by burning the
effigy of a person, either to his honour, or in
deifying him, or else in public detestation of
some high and notorious crime and misdemeanor.
Sometimes they burnt living persons themselves,
(even for pleasure, on their public feast days) to
the honour of their gods, and the mirth and
jovialty of their barbarous spectators. Thus Nero
wrapt the Christians in hemp and pitch, and
made them serve as torches to his theatre ; in
contempt (as some write) of that saying, *Ye are
the lights of the world.*

Many persons are of opinion, that the religious principles of the Druids were similar to
those of the Gymnosophists and Brahmans of
India, the Magi of Persia, and the Chaldeans of
Assyria, and therefore to have the same origin ;
which opinion appears well grounded, and cre-
dited by the learned of several countries.

The Gymnosophists were philosophers who
went naked, and lived solitary and austere lives,
in caves, woods, and desarts, feeding on herbs,
and for a time abstaining from carnal pleasures.
They were also called Brahmans or Bramins, of
Brachman or Bramba, the prescriber of their
rights or laws. They were very learned men,
held in great reverence by the people, and had
a strong idea of the Trinity, their opinion being,
that the god Achari or Wistan created the world
by the administration of three perfect beings,
whom he had first made for that design : these
three are, 1st, Bramba, (viz. Penetration) by
this he created the universe :—

2d, Breschen, (viz. existing in all things);
by this he preserves it :—

3d, Mahaddia, (viz. the great Lord); by this he will destroy it.

They pretend to have received four books from Bramba, in which books all knowledge is comprehended; they acknowledge the metampsychosis, or transmigration of souls, through several human bodies and beasts, before they can arrive at pleasure and being purely spiritual: and for this reason they teach, that it is not lawful to kill, or eat any thing that is killed, and none of their tribes do eat any, but their soldiers. They also hold the flesh of cows and peacocks as sacred, and therefore they abstain from it; and build hospitals for lame and decayed beasts, and buy birds of the Mahometans to set them at liberty. By their austere lives, great fastings, teaching the people, and expounding the mysteries of their religion to them, they have obtained a very great awe over the people in the Indies, and especially upon the Malabar coasts: and the brides are committed to the Bramins, to be blessed by them, that the marriage may be happy.

Now the Druids held the metampsychosis, though they destroyed so many human and animal beings; and they thought it was not lawful to eat ducks or hens, and many other winged animals. They, like the other priests just mentioned, kept many of their opinions secret, and taught the others publicly. Whatever opinions they privately entertained, in public they worshipped a multiplicity of deities.

Many of their mysteries, it is said, are contained in the Hebrew word *Elohim*, which implies very different meanings. Mr. HUTCHINSON says it signifies strength, power, and the Covenants, or ever-blessed Trinity, being one God,

JEHOVAH. From that word they think it plain, that not only their kind of worship in woods and groves was at first derived, but that the whole of the Trinity is deducible from a right understanding of it.

They had also different manners of worshipping their various deities, and a particular sacrifice for every one. The names of their chief gods were, Jupiter, Tutates, and Hesus, to whom they offered most of their human victims.

The usage of performing all their acts of worship in the open air or uncovered temples, comes from their opinion that it derogated from the greatness of the gods to confine them within close places, or to assimulate them to any human form.

There is no doubt but they had the same gods as the Gauls, and agreed with them in their manner of worship: neither indeed could it be otherwise, if we consider what care they took to preserve the unity of religion, and the exact observances of their order: for besides the yearly synods held in the isles of Anglesey and Man, under their Primate or Arch-Druid, they had a solemn and general sessions, in a field set apart for that purpose, near Drew, in Pays Chartrin, the chief residence of the Arch-Druid of Gaul, who had in the neighbourhood another palace among woods.

To this great assembly resorted the Druids from all parts, to hear causes, and to consult about the affairs of religion, in which consultation the British Druids, it is said, carried the most eminent authority; they also agreed upon the number of their gods, and the particular honors due to them: they instituted public feasts and sacrifices upon set times of the moon, that the day might be celebrated uniformly through all their jurisdictions.

Though they had a fixed number of gods, yet in many particular places, the people had private and tutelar gods, whose denominations extended not beyond a hill, river, fountain, or spring.

Jupiter was worshipped under many names, and indeed, as VARRO says, we read of above 300 Jupiters, and each nation seems to have had one peculiar to itself. He who was worshipped in Britain, was, without any doubt, the Jove of the eastern nations, finding his names and worship the same exactly as in these western parts.

He was particularly called Taramis, viz. Thunderer; and Thor, in the north, which name signifies also Thunder; and from which is derived Thursday, viz. the day of Thor, because that day out of the seven in the week was consecrated to him. The Swedes, Germans, and Saxons, worshipped him in the same manner as the Britons and Gauls; we therefore need but relate the divine honors paid to him in our island.

He was looked upon as the cause of life —source of enlivening fire—father of gods and men: called, the omnipotent—the first and the last—the head and the middle—the giver of all things—the foundation of the earth and starry heavens—and he was believed to be both male and female, and immortal.

He was held to rule and govern the air; they thought that from him proceeded thunder and lightning, winds and storms—that he gave fair weather, and brought forward the fruits of the earth. The Phœnicians called him Moloch;

viz. the king of the gods. Some say Moloch
was the same with Saturn; others with Noah.
It is observable, that as the Canaanites (of which
country Phœnicia was a part) offered human
sacrifices to that god, so likewise did the Gauls
and Britons to their Taramis or Thunderer.

The Canaanites, the Egyptians, the inhabitants of Palestine, and many other people,
offered their own children unto him; and the
Israelites themselves imitated their barbarities.
They caused their children to pass between two
fires, till they were miserably scorched: they
also shut them up in a hollow idol of brass,
representing Moloch, made red hot; and while
these innocent victims were in this manner tormented, they sounded trumpets, beat drums,
&c. to drown their cries.

Upon the altars erected in honour of Jupiter, the British blood was often poured out in
great abundance; but perhaps more in Gaul,
because that country being more infected with
sudden thunders and violent storms, they
oftener atoned that power under whose hand
they lay, than the Britons, who enjoyed a more
temperate and serene air.

These customs, together with the name of
this god Taramis, were brought in by the Phœnicians, who are described by HAVILLAN, the
poet, (writing of their race in Cornwall) that
their Spectacula, or public games, in honour of
their gods, was the slaughter of men, and not
only so, but they drank their blood. Neither
did the Druids, who were in other respects men
of civil and upright conversation, alter these
bloody ceremonies, because most of them came
out of Greece in those early days when the sacrificing of men and women existed there.

## Description of the Druidical Temples, &c.

Near the Main Ambre, at Penzance, is a famous patriarchal temple, called Biscawoon, consisting of 19 pillars in a circle and a central Kebla: the entrance composed of two larger stones than the rest.

These patriarchal or druidical temples were laid out in such figures as were hieroglyphical, and intended to describe the nature of the Divinity; as the Circle, such is that of Stonehenge; or the Circle and Seraph, or winged Serpent, as that of Abiry.

That the temples of this sort which we have amongst us were really founded by the people to whom they are now ascribed, will be further evident from a consideration of the works themselves: the measures of every one of which are observed to fall easily and naturally in round and full numbers into the scale of Phœnician or Hebrew cubits. Nor will they admit of the standard measure of Greece or Rome, or any Western nation, without being divided and broken into infinite and trifling fractions.

To illustrate what has been advanced, we shall give as brief a description as can be of the two famous ones already mentioned in this neighbourhood. We shall begin with Abiry, as the more ancient work of the two.

Abiry is founded on the more elevated part of a plain, whence is an almost imperceptible descent every way. The entire figure of it, is a Seraph or winged Serpent transmitted through a circle. The outer part of the grand circle is a vast and lofty vallum, with a very deep ditch on the inside of it, near 80 feet or 45 cubits broad. Its diameter 750 cubits; its circumference 2250 cubits; the inclosed area about 22 acres.

Within this ditch was formed a circle of 100 enormous stones set upright; which were generally 15, 16, or 17 feet high, and near as much in breadth. Twenty-five cubits is the regular measure with regard to the larger stones from the centre of the one to the centre of the other, making the interval 15 cubits. But in all of them throughout, the proportion of the solid to the void is as 2 to 3. Out of these 100 stones 44 were still visible when Dr. Stukeley was there in the year 1722; whereof 17 were standing and 27 thrown down or reclining. Ten of the remainder had been demolished by Tom Robinson in the year 1700, and their places levelled. The vestigia of the rest were still discernible. When this mighty colonade of 100 such stones was in perfection, there must have been a most agreeable walk between them and the ditch. It is scarcely possible for us to form a notion of the grand and beautiful appearance it must then have made.

Within this circle were the Wings, being two temples of like form and dimensions; each consisting of two concentric circles. The outer circles contain each 30 stones of like dimensions and placed at like intervals with those already mentioned. The inner circles of both consist each of 12 stones of the same size and distances. The inner circle must therefore be 100 cubits in diameter; the outer 250 cubits. So that the Periphery of the outer circles of the wings is equal to the diameter of the great circle.

The southermost of these temples has a central obelisk which was the Kibla whereto they turned their faces in worship. The other has that immense work in the centre, which the Hebrews or Phœnicians called *Kobhe*, and from them the Old Britons a Cove: consisting of three stones placed with an obtuse angle towards each other, and as it were upon an arc of a circle, like the great half round at the east end of some cathedrals. It was the Adytum of this temple and the Kibla thereof, opening north-east: the extravagant magnitude and majesty of which is very astonishing. It measures 20 cubits from the edge of the outer jambs, and 10 cubits in depth. Upon the ground before this superb nitch lay the altar, which no doubt was carried off long ago, as not being fixed; and the northern pillar is also gone: it fell down in the year 1713. Its length was seven yards, of the same shape with its opposite, tall and narrow. This measured 17 feet above ground, being 10 whole cubits; 4 cubits broad, and 1 cubit and a half thick. Such were the Ansæ or wings of this noble ellipsis. That in the middle is 9 cubits broad, as many high, and 2 cubits and a half thick. Of the exterior circle of this northern temple, but three are now left standing, and six more lying on the ground. In 1720, both circles were standing and almost entire. About that time several stones of the southern temple were destroyed; but 14 are still left, whereof about half are standing. The central obelisk of this temple is circular at the base ; of a vast bulk, being 12 cubits long, and 5 cubits in diameter ; and standing higher than the rest. Formerly it was the altar of this temple. Most of the houses, walls, and outhouses of this town are built with the materials of these stones that have been fired and broken. Under an ash tree dug here was found one of the Druids axes or Celts, wherewith they cut the misletoe of the oak.

Let us walk out now by the southern entrance of the town, passing the vallum : the road straight forward leads to Kennet and Overton. This is the *Via sacra*, being an avenue up to the temple, and forming besides one half of the body of the Seraph. This was more than an English mile, and set with stones on both sides opposite to one another and at regular distances. As this was to be the picture of an animal, the Druids followed nature's drawing as nearly as possible, making the avenue narrower towards the neck than at its middle. The whole length of it consists of 100 stones on each side, reaching from the vallum of Abiry town to the circular work upon Overton Hill. The same proportion is every where preserved between breadth and interval as before. Mounting up Overton Hill, the avenue grows much narrower. In 1722 the number of stones left were 72.

In a field on the left hand, or east of the avenue, not far from Abiry town, is a pentagonal stone laid flat on the ground, in the middle of which is a bason always full, and never overflowing, much regarded by the country people, and proceeding from a spring underneath ; which may have been here from the foundation of the temple, for purifications.

The summit of Overton Hill is the Hak-pen, (a compound oriental word signifying the serpent's head), which is 4000 cubits from the vallum of Abiry. This hill the people have a high notion of, and still call it the sanctuary. Unfortunately all the stones have been removed, and the ground ploughed up. The stones here were not large, but set pretty close together; and the proportions of them with the intervals and between the two circles, all taken at one view, charmed the spectator. Many people here remember both circles entire and standing, two or three fallen stones excepted, and they are still talked of with great pleasure and regret The outer circle consisted of 40 stones, and the inner of 18, somewhat larger than the others. From Overton Hill is a most pleasing prospect, overlooking the whole extent of the temple and sacred field, and beyond that into Glocestershire and Somersetshire.

We now proceed to Bekhampton Avenue, which extends also 4000 cubits, or an eastern mile from Abiry towards Bekhampton. It is the hinder part of the hieroglyphic Seraph, which the Druids thus pourtrayed in this most portentous size; and the number of the stones, as of the other, was 100 on each side; but almost all of them have been destroyed and carried away. Yet the unwearied industry of Dr. Stukeley has traced out the Obit of every stone. It goes out of Abiry westward at the interval of 25 stones, or a quadrant of the great circle at Kennet Avenue, and proceeds by the south side of the church-yard. A little spring rises at Horslip north-west, and flows thence to Silbury Hill, where is the proper head of the Kennet; and sometimes this is very deep. The picture here humours the reality so far, that this may properly be called the vent of the animal. When you come to the fiftieth stone on the north side, is a magnificent Cove, like that already described : the stone of the avenue making the back stone of the Cove. This served for an oratory to the neighbourhood upon ordinary days of devotion. It is placed on the highest ground which this avenue occupies, and the grounds have gained from it the name of Longstone Fields. Only one of the stones is now standing, which is 9 cubits high, as many broad, and 2 cubits thick. The back stone is flat on the ground, and of the same dimensions. The other was carried off when Dr. STUKELEY was there, and contained, when broken, twenty good loads. This avenue terminates near a groupe of barrows under Cherril Hill, in the way to Oldbury Camp, west of Bekhampton. This point, facing that groupe of barrows and looking up the hill, is a most solemn and awful place : a descent all the way from Longstone Cove and directed to a descent a great way further, down the Bath road, where no less than five valleys meet. The end of it drew narrower in imitation of the tail, which was closed by one stone in the middle.

The Druids were tempted to draw out this stupendous work in such manner, by the appearance of the surprising multitude of stones on the Downs, called the Grey Wethers, and which at a distance resemble a flock of sheep : six hundred and fifty two of the choicest of which were conveyed hither to make this noble temple.

Such was this wonderful work of Abiry, than which a grander and more extensive design scarce ever entered into the imagination of man; and which, when in perfection, was without question the most glorious temple of the kind which the world has ever heard of. That it was really a temple sacred to the ever-blessed and undivided Trinity, every circumstance, every consideration tends to persuade us ; and one particularly which has not yet been attended to, and that is the name itself of Abiry (ABIRI, *Potentes*), signifying in the language of its founders, The Mighty Ones ; of whom the whole was an emblematical representation.

Its situation is in a country full of wonders, where there is great scope for the contemplative and the curious. It is all a healthy rock of chalk, covered with pure virgin turf, the encroachments of the avaricious plough excepted. Eastward are the Downs, still called Temple Downs : westward the camp of Oldbury. On the south that prodigious barrow known by the name of Silbury Hill, besides a multitude of others. Then the *Via Badonica* or Roman Way. Further on is that astonishing line of Wandsdyke, supposed to have been drawn by the Belgæ, to secure the conquests they made in Britain, before the time of Julius Cæsar. Next, hills, emerging from the fruitful and delicious vale below, which emulate the clouds, some of them capt with barrows, and so made more superb monuments than the pyramids of Egypt. Hence you see the wide extent of Salisbury Plain, and the cathedral of Sarum at the distance of near thirty miles. The air is fine and invigorating ; and the prospect, which way soever you turn, seems all enchantment, and dilates the heart beyond expression.

We shall now proceed to Stonehenge, which is not erected upon the very summit of a hill, but pretty near; and for more than three quarters of the circuit you ascend to it very gently from lower ground; but from the north the ascent is quicker. It is composed of two circles and two ovals respectively concentric. And the greatness of the lights and shades, as well as their variety arising from the circular figure, gives it all possible advantage. The whole is inclosed by a circular ditch, originally 30 cubits broad, but now levelled very much. The distance between the verge of the ditch on the inside, quite round, to the work of the temple, is equal to the diameter of the temple itself, viz. 60 cubits : so that the entire diameter from the outer verge of the ditch is 240 cubits.

When you enter the building and cast your eyes around upon the yawning ruins, you are struck into an extatic reverie, which none can describe, and they only can be sensible of that feel it. Other buildings fall by piecemeal, but here a single stone is a ruin. Yet is there as much of it left undemolished, as enables us very sufficiently to recover its pristine form. The best face of the stone is set inward; and those that had the best outward face, toward the front or entrance.

The intention of the founders was this: the whole outer circle was to consist of 30 upright stones; each stone was to be 4 cubits broad; each interval 2 cubits. But the grand aperture is 2 cubits and a half wide: this crouds the next intervals on each side a little nearer; the rest preserving their true distance throughout.

Upon the top of these 30 uprights were

placed an equal number of imposts, secured with mortise and tenon, in such a manner that the whole circle is linked together in a continued corona, by the imposts or cornice being carried quite round. The centres of the tenons are two cubits distant from each other upon each upright and fit the mortises very aptly. They are rather a semi-oval than a hemisphere. The height of upright and impost is 10 cubits and a half, of which the upright is nine; so that the impost is a sixth part of the height of the upright: but as the entrance is wider, so the impost over it is thicker than the rest to secure it from breaking. If we measure on the outside the collective breadth of two uprights and the interval between them, it is 10 cubits and a half, equal to the whole height. The interval is half the breadth of a stone; and the thickness of a stone is half its breadth.

Of the uprights there are 17 yet standing, 11 of which remain contiguous to the grand entrance, with 5 imposts upon them. One upright more, at the back of the temple or on the south-west, leans upon a stone of the inner circle. There are six more lying upon the ground, whole or in pieces; so that 24 out of 30 are still visible at the place. There is but one impost more in its proper place, and but two lying on the ground; so that 22 are carried off.

Through the middle of the principal entrance runs the principal line of the whole work, the diameter from north-east to south-west. This line cuts the middle of the altar, the length of the Adytum or cell, the entrance into the court, and so runs down the middle of the avenue to the bottom of the valley for almost 2000 feet. This is very apparent at first sight,

and determines this for the principal entrance.
Upon this line are all the principal centres that
compose the work : it varies a little from true
north-east.

Five cubits inward from the inside of this
exterior circle, is another of much smaller
stones. A radius of 23 cubits strikes the inner
circumference; of 24 the outer. The stones
that composed it were 40 in number; forming
with the outer circle a very noble and delightful
walk, 300 feet in circuit. They are a cubit
thick and 4 cubits and a half high. This was
their stated proportion, being every way the
half of the outer uprights. Such seems to have
been the original purpose of the founders; though
in some places the stones are broader than the
intervals, and in some otherwise. There are
scarce any of these entire as to all their dimensions. The central distance of these stones,
measured upon their outer circumference, is
4 cubits : those two which form the principal
entrance of this circle, correspondent to that of
the outer circle, are broader and taller, and farther distant from each other. They are also set
so much farther inward, that the outer face of
them runs in a line with the inner face of the
others, and eminently points out the principal
entrance. There are but 19 of the whole number left ; but 11 of them are standing, and five
particularly in one place contiguous.

The Adytum or cell, which presents itself
next, is a most noble and beautiful ellipsis; nor
is there any thing like it in all antiquity. It is
an original invention of the Druids, an inge-
nious contrivance to relax the inner and more
sacred part, where they performed their religious
offices. The two outer circles were no disad-

vantage to the view from hence, but added much
to the solemnity of the place and of the duties
discharged in it, by the frequency and variety
of their intervals. They that were within, when
it was in perfection, would see a fine effect produced by this elliptical figure included in a circular corona, having a large hemisphere of the
heavens for its covering.

The exterior oval is composed of certain
compages of stones, which Dr. STUKELEY calls
Trilithons, being made each of two uprights
with an impost at top. The interior curve is
formed by a radius of 12 cubits and a half from
two centres; the outer by one of fifteen cubits;
the stones being two cubits and a half thick.
Their height and breadth is also enormous; and
to see so many of them placed together in a nice
and critical figure—to consider, not a pillar, but
a whole wall, a side, an end of a temple, of one
stone, creates such emotion in the mind as is
not easy to be expressed. The uprights are each
4 cubits and a half broad at the bottom, but
grow narrower towards the top, in order to lessen
their weight. This widens the interval, but
contributes very much to their stability. Each
Trilithon is ten cubits, and each interval about
six. Of these there are five in number; three
of which are entire. Two are ruined indeed in
some measure, but the stones remain in their
place, as this part of the work is the most perfect
of the whole. That at the upper end is exceeding
stately, though in ruins; one of the uprights
having fallen, the other leaning. As you look
from the grand entrance towards the altar, the
jambs of the two hithermost Trilithons present
themselves with a magnificent opening 25 cubits
wide. One remarkable particular in the con-

struction of this oval is, that the two hithermost Trilithons corresponding, (viz. next the grand entrance on the right hand and on the left), are exceeded in height by the two next in order, and those by the Trilithon behind the altar ; thus improving in height and beauty from the lower to the upper end of the choir. Hence their respective heights are 13, 14, and 15 cubits.

The stones of the interior oval are placed 2 cubits from the other. They were 19 in number, at about the central distance of 3 cubits : each stone being a cubit and a half broad, and the interval the same. Their height is unequal, like that of the Trilithons, rising higher towards the upper end of the Adytum : at a medium, it is 8 feet, or 4 cubits and 4 palms. From the ruins of those left, we may well suppose that the first next the entrance and lowest were 4 cubits high ; and the most advanced height behind the altar might be 5 cubits, and perhaps more. These stones are in form somewhat like an Egyptian obelisk, tapering a little upwards. They are much harder than the rest, as are the stones in the lesser circle before described ; so that what is wanting in bulk is compensated in solidity. Of these there are only six remaining upright : the stumps of two are left on the south side by the altar : one lies behind the altar, dug up, or thrown down by the fall of the upright there. One or two were thrown down probably by the fall of the upright of the first Trilithon on the right hand : and the stump of another remains by the upright there, still standing.

The altar is of a blue, coarse, and firm marble, as designed to resist fire, placed a little above the focus of the upper end of the ellipsis ;

four feet broad, 16 feet long, and 20 inches thick; leaving round it room sufficient for the ministration of the priests.

The whole number of stones of which this most superb temple was composed, is 140.

It has already been observed that the avenue of the temple runs in a line north-eastward from the grand entrance. It is inclosed all the way by two parrallel ditches, the earth and turf of which was thrown inward, and the avenue by that means raised above the common level of the plain. The breadth of it from ditch to ditch is 40 cubits: from the entrance of the area to the valley beneath is just 1000 cubits. Thence it divides into two branches: the right-hand branch winding till it shoots directly east, towards an ancient ford of the river, called Radfin Ford; the left-hand branch goes off with a similar sweep at first, but does not throw itself into a direct line, as the other, but continues curving to the left along the bottom of the hill, till it loses itself in the Course or Hippodrome.

This Course or Hippodrome is also inclosed between two ditches, 200 cubits asunder; the earth of which was also thrown inward and the turf raised. It is two English miles, or 6000 cubits in length, and has two opposite en-entrances. It lies directly north from Stonehenge, at the distance of about half a mile, and is drawn due east and west, a small variation excepted. The west end of it, towards which are many considerable barrows, is curved into an arch, for the convenience of turning the contending chariots. Its eastern termination is shut up with a long bank or huge mole of earth, where the judges of the race are supposed to have sat; and whence they had a distinct view of all that was transacted within the compass of this magnificent Course.

The compilers of the Universal History insist that Stonehenge is not a temple, but a monument. The reason given by them is, " Because we have many convincing arguments " that neither Celtes, nor Gauls and Britons " had any such buildings, till long after the " coming of the Romans." Yet the same authors commend Dr. STUKELEY's observations as judicious, which says, that Choir Gaur, its ancient name, might properly be rendered the Great Church, or Grand Choir. They also allow that it answers to the notion of a temple by reason of its sacredness, its resemblance to the ancient religious groves, and the sacrifices and other rites performed there. It answers to that of a sepulchral monument, on account of its being appropriated to the grandest funeral ceremonies, and its being the centre or Kibla to all the adjacent monuments round about ; to that of an amphitheatre, on account of the funeral games and shows exhibited at it ; and may also have served for a convening place of the national council, &c.

And indeed, that it answered all these purposes, will appear evident to every considering person. Probably none of the ancient inhabitants of these islands might have temples, in the modern acceptation of the term, covered and regularly inclosed as afterwards : but wherever an altar was placed, public sacrifices offered, and the Deity invoked, though there was nothing else, or but a single pillar set up for a Kibla, that place was properly a patriarchal temple.

That the barrows within sight of it have relation to Stonehenge—that sacrifices might be

offered and religious offices there performed, and
sports exhibited at some distance at the celebration of each great funeral, is readily granted.
Yet surely all this does not oppose, but rather
confirm, the notion of its having been a temple.
Religiously disposed persons are generally de-
sirous of being interred near the places of religious worship; which is an expression of their
assent to that worship, and of their confidence
in the object of it. But what relation to Stonehenge have the barrows thrown up about War-
minster, at the distance of fifteen or twenty
miles? And what those which are far on the
other side the river by Everley and Collinbourne,
and even in the valley about Tottenham, at a
considerable distance from the plain itself?

To the meeting of great assemblies, whether
on religious or civil accounts, the place seems
peculiarly adapted; for which purpose the world
does not afford a nobler spot. Its situation is
upon a hill, in the midst of an extended plain
100 miles in circuit, in the centre of the southern
part of the kingdom, covered with numberless
flocks of herds and sheep, in which respect the
employment and the plains themselves are patriarchal; where the air is perfectly salubrious
and exhilirating, and the yielding turf fine as
the surface of a bowling-green. From almost
every adjoining eminence the prospect is open
into Hampshire, Dorsetshire, Somersetshire, and
takes in all the lofty hills between Marlborough
and Sandy-Lane, sustaining the long range of
Wandsdyke and the mother church of Abiry.

In such a consecrated place, in the territory
of the Carnutes, the centre of Gaul, at a certain
season of the year the Druids of that country
were wont to meet; where and by whom all

controversies were settled, and whose judgments and decisions were readily obeyed. Their discipline they obtained from Britain, whither those who were willing to learn it, still went for instruction.

FINIS.

LOMAX, PRINTER, LICHFIELD.

www.ingramcontent.com/pod-product-compliance
Lightning Source LLC
LaVergne TN
LVHW012201040326
832903LV00003B/55

*  9  7  8  1  0  1  7  1  5  3  8  8  0  *